CW00536188

THE LITTLE BOOK OF . . .

Yasmine Sobhi

Grosvenor House
Publishing Limited

This book is published by
Grosvenor House Publishing Ltd
Link House
140 The Broadway, Tolworth, Surrey, KT6 7HT.
www.grosvenorhousepublishing.co.uk

This book is a work of fiction. Any resemblance to
people or events, past or present, is purely coincidental.

A CIP record for this book
is available from the British Library

ISBN 978-1-80381-505-3

DEDICATION

TO MY CRAZY FAMILY, MY SECOND MUM
AND ULTIMATELY TO MYSELF & EVERYONE
WHO READS THIS BOOK THIS IS A MESSAGE
TO YOU, FOLLOW YOUR LIGHT AND YOU
WILL FOREVER SHINE BRIGHT.

I LOVE YOU; ♥

CONTENTS OF THIS BOOK

POEMS ABOUT LOVE...
LIFE
HAPPINESS
PATIENCE
PEACE
FOUR LINE-ART PICTURES SPREAD THROUGHOUT
THE BOOK IN A UNIQUELY BEAUTIFUL ORDER
THAT TELLS ITS OWN STORY.
PERSONAL THOUGHTS JOURNAL
FAVOURITE QUOTES

YASMINE SOBHI

– LUCKY IS YOU BECAUSE THIS BOOK CHOSE YOU,
NOW LET'S READ THROUGH. –

GRANTED WISH

THE MOON MAY BE BRIGHT,
THE MOON THAT GIVES US LIGHT,
I PRAY THAT I MAY
AND I PRAY THAT I MIGHT
JUST HAVE MY WISH GRANTED
ON THIS BEAUTIFUL NIGHT.

WHAT DID THIS POEM MEAN TO YOU
AND WHY?

. . . .

. . . .

. . . .

. . . .

SET YOUR HEART'S INTENTION FOR TODAY

. . . .

. . . .

. . . .

. . . .

SELFLESSNESS

SOMEONE ONCE TOLD ME,
DO NOT GIVE ALL OF YOU,
BUT INSTEAD GIVE HALF OF YOU.
WHY?
BECAUSE THE HALF THAT YOU KEEP
WILL HELP REPLENISH
THE HALF THAT YOU GIVE.

WHAT DID THIS POEM MEAN TO YOU
AND WHY?

....

....

....

....

SET YOUR HEART'S INTENTION FOR TODAY

....

....

....

....

"THOSE WHO HAVE
CONQUERED WARS OF THE MIND
WIELD THE MOST
POWERFUL WEAPON OF ALL,
COURAGE."

OLIVIA ANN ROSE

HEART'S DESIRE

I LOVE YOU I DO,
BELIEVE ME THAT'S TRUE,
I WOULD DO ANYTHING
JUST TO HAVE YOU,
SO I COULD VALUE EVERY
MOMENT THAT I GOT TO SPEND
SITTING RIGHT NEXT TO
YOU.

WHAT DID THIS POEM MEAN TO YOU
AND WHY?

. . . .

. . . .

. . . .

. . . .

SET YOUR HEART'S INTENTION FOR TODAY

. . . .

. . . .

. . . .

. . . .

"BEAUTY IS NOT
IN THE FACE;
BEAUTY IS A LIGHT
IN THE HEART."

KHALIL GIBRAN

TIME'S LIMITED

TIME KEEPS RUNNING
THE CLOCKS KEEP TICKING,
PEOPLE ARE HERE
THEN PEOPLE ARE THERE
BUT BREATHE IN THAT FEAR,
WIPE THAT TEAR
WATCH EVERYTHING
SUDDENLY SEEM ALL
CLEAR.

WHAT DID THIS POEM MEAN TO YOU
AND WHY?

. . . .

. . . .

. . . .

. . . .

SET YOUR HEART'S INTENTION FOR TODAY

. . . .

. . . .

. . . .

. . . .

HEALER

SOMETIMES I SIT AND I WONDER,
WHY DO I FEEL
WHAT OTHERS THINK THEY CONCEAL,
THEN I REALISE
I FEEL SO DEEPLY
SO THAT I CAN HELP
HEAL.

WHAT DID THIS POEM MEAN TO YOU
AND WHY?

. . . .

. . . .

. . . .

. . . .

SET YOUR HEART'S INTENTION FOR TODAY

. . . .

. . . .

. . . .

. . . .

"SOMETIMES YOU WILL NEVER KNOW
THE VALUE OF A
MOMENT
UNTIL IT BECOMES A
MEMORY."

DR SEUSS

DIAMONDS IN THE DUST

I MAY NOT BE LIKEABLE TO EVERYONE
NOR DO I WANT TO BE,
WHAT I AM IS VALUABLE,
REMEMBER WHAT IS VALUED
IS NOT LIKED BY PLENTY
BUT TREASURED
BY FEW.

WHAT DID THIS POEM MEAN TO YOU
AND WHY?

. . . .

. . . .

. . . .

. . . .

SET YOUR HEART'S INTENTION FOR TODAY

. . . .

. . . .

. . . .

. . . .

"I'VE LEARNED THAT PEOPLE
WILL FORGET WHAT YOU
SAID,
PEOPLE WILL FORGET WHAT YOU
DID,
BUT PEOPLE WILL NEVER FORGET
HOW YOU MADE THEM
FEEL."

MAYA ANGELOU

PATIENCE IS STRENGTH

PATIENCE... SOMETHING WE ALL
STRIVE FOR BUT VERY FEW HAVE,
PATIENCE IS OFTEN
MISUNDERSTOOD
IT'S NOT ABOUT HOW LONG
YOU WAIT FOR SOMETHING
BUT RATHER
HOW WE ACT
IN THE TIME WE ARE
PATIENTLY WAITING.

WHAT DID THIS POEM MEAN TO YOU
AND WHY?

. . . .

. . . .

. . . .

. . . .

SET YOUR HEART'S INTENTION FOR TODAY

. . . .

. . . .

. . . .

. . . .

"SOME OF THE BEST ADVICE
I'VE BEEN GIVEN:
'DON'T TAKE CRITICISM FROM
PEOPLE
YOU WOULD NEVER GO TO
FOR ADVICE'."

MORGAN FREEMAN

"YOUR PATIENCE
IS YOUR
POWER."

K. TOLNOE

"EVERY PROBLEM
IS A GIFT –
WITHOUT PROBLEMS
WE WOULD NOT
GROW."

TONY ROBBINS

AWARENESS

WORDS ARE THE MOST POWRFUL TOOL
WE OFTEN DON'T TAKE CARE OF
WHEN USING,
SO USE WISELY
USE CAREFULLY
AND USE
LOVINGLY,
BECAUSE AT THE END
WHAT WE SPEAK
IS WHAT WE BECOME.

WHAT DID THIS POEM MEAN TO YOU
AND WHY?

. . . .

. . . .

. . . .

. . . .

SET YOUR HEART'S INTENTION FOR TODAY

. . . .

. . . .

. . . .

. . . .

INNER HAPPINESS IS LIFE'S KEY

YOU SEE HAPPINESS
TO ME
ISN'T LAUGHING AND FEELING
JOYFUL WHEN YOU'RE SURROUNDED
BY PEOPLE,
BUT RATHER
FEELING AT PEACE
AND TRUE GRATITUDE
WHEN YOU'RE ALONE,
YOU SEE
WHEN WE'RE ALONE
THAT IS WHEN WE'RE TRULY
KNOWN.

WHAT DID THIS POEM MEAN TO YOU
AND WHY?

. . . .

. . . .

. . . .

. . . .

SET YOUR HEART'S INTENTION FOR TODAY

. . . .

. . . .

. . . .

. . . .

"WHEN THEY HURT YOU, HURTING THEM
BACK
WILL NOT HEAL
YOUR PAIN.
INSTEAD TREAT THEM KINDLY. RISE
ABOVE IT ALL AND DO GOOD.
ALWAYS LEAVE A TRAIL OF GOODNESS.
LET THE ALMIGHTY HANDLE THE REST.
HE WILL NOT ONLY REWARD YOU FOR YOUR
EFFORTS,
HE WILL ALSO HEAL YOU."

ISMAIL IBN MUSA MENK

MY POWER

PEOPLE OFTEN ASK ME
WHY I'M ALWAYS HAPPY,
THE ANSWER IS SIMPLE
I AM HAPPY
BECAUSE I AM GRATEFUL,
AND I AM GRATEFUL
NOT BECAUSE I DON'T HAVE
PROBLEMS,
BUT BECAUSE I
EMBRACE MY PROBLEMS,
AND FOR THAT
I WILL ALWAYS
REMAIN AND RECLAIM
MY HAPPINESS.

WHAT DID THIS POEM MEAN TO YOU
AND WHY?

. . . .

. . . .

. . . .

. . . .

SET YOUR HEART'S INTENTION FOR TODAY

. . . .

. . . .

. . . .

. . . .

"WHETHER YOU THINK
YOU CAN
OR YOU THINK
YOU CAN'T,
YOU'RE RIGHT."

HENRY FORD

DON'T TURN A BLIND EYE

SOMETIMES
THE WORLD FEELS LIKE
IT'S TOO MUCH TO BEAR,
BUT...
IF WE FILTER THROUGH THE AIR
AND SHOW WE CARE
WE MIGHT
JUST BE ABLE
TO REPAIR.

WHAT DID THIS POEM MEAN TO YOU
AND WHY?

. . . .

. . . .

. . . .

. . . .

SET YOUR HEART'S INTENTION FOR TODAY

. . . .

. . . .

. . . .

. . . .

NEVER ALONE

LIFE CAN SOMETIMES
SEEM DARK AND FULL OF DESPAIR,
IN THOSE MOMENTS
WHEN YOU'RE GRASPING
FOR A BREATH OF
FRESH AIR,
KNOW THAT
YOU
ARE WORTHY AND EVER SO CARED,
SO TAKE MY HAND
AND HOLD IT TIGHT
AND I PROMISE
YOU CAN MAKE IT THROUGH THIS
FIGHT.

WHAT DID THIS POEM MEAN TO YOU
AND WHY?

. . . .

. . . .

. . . .

. . . .

SET YOUR HEART'S INTENTION FOR TODAY

. . . .

. . . .

. . . .

. . . .

"IF YOU HEAR A VOICE WITHIN
YOU SAY
'YOU CANNOT PAINT',
THEN BY ALL
MEANS PAINT
AND THAT VOICE WILL BE
SILENCED."

VINCENT VAN GOGH

"YOUR TIME IS LIMITED,
SO DON'T WASTE IT
LIVING SOMEONE
ELSE'S LIFE."

STEVE JOBS

YOU ARE ALREADY WINNING

I'M SENDING YOU A HUG
PLEASE KNOW YOU ARE
LOVED,
THROUGH UPS AND DOWNS
LEFTS AND RIGHTS,
TWISTS AND TURNS,
HURTS AND BURNS,
YOU ARE TOUGH
PLEASE KNOW YOU ARE
ENOUGH.

WHAT DID THIS POEM MEAN TO YOU
AND WHY?

. . . .

. . . .

. . . .

. . . .

SET YOUR HEART'S INTENTION FOR TODAY

. . . .

. . . .

. . . .

. . . .

"AN EYE FOR AN EYE
WILL ONLY MAKE THE
WHOLE WORLD
BLIND."

MAHATMA GANDHI

"NEVER MIND WHAT
OTHERS DO;
DO BETTER THAN
YOURSELF,
BEAT YOUR OWN RECORD,
EACH AND EVERY DAY,
AND YOU ARE
A SUCCESS."

WILLIAM BOETCKER

MY HUG FROM YOU

SUNSETS ARE MAGICAL
THROUGH AND THROUGH,
WHENEVER I LOOK UP,
I THINK OF YOU,
AND I FEEL YOUR LIGHT
SHINING THROUGH
IT FEELS JUST LIKE
A HUG
STRAIGHT FROM YOU,
JUST KNOW
I MISS YOU TOO.

WHAT DID THIS POEM MEAN TO YOU
AND WHY?

....

....

....

....

SET YOUR HEART'S INTENTION FOR TODAY

....

....

....

....

"THE BEST AND MOST
BEAUTIFUL THINGS IN THE WORLD
CANNOT BE SEEN OR
EVEN TOUCHED –
THEY MUST BE FELT
WITH THE HEART."

HELEN KELLER

BACK TO MOTHER NATURE

I LOVE TO BE STILL FOR A FEW MINUTES
EVERY DAY,
NO PHONE,
NO LAPTOP,
NO PEOPLE,
JUST ME, MY THOUGHTS AND NATURE
CONNECT AND REENERGISE
AND SOON WE REALISE
AS WE RECONNECT
WE GROW AND AS WE GROW
WE FLOURISH INTO
THE BEST VERSIONS
OF OURSELVES
FOR OURSELVES AND
WITH OURSELVES.

WHAT DID THIS POEM MEAN TO YOU
AND WHY?

. . . .

. . . .

. . . .

. . . .

SET YOUR HEART'S INTENTION FOR TODAY

. . . .

. . . .

. . . .

. . . .

I WONDER

THERE'S SOMETHING SPECIAL
AND INTRIGUING
THAT LEAVES ME FEELING
ALMOST LIKE THERE'S MORE
OF A MEANING
BEHIND EVERYTHING THAT I'M READING,
SO I ASK YOU,
DO YOU HAVE THE SAME FEELING!
I HOPE YOU AS THE PERSON READING
FINDS YOUR OWN MEANING
SO YOU CAN START ACHIEVING
EVERYTHING THAT YOU'VE BEEN
DREAMING
AND LET PEOPLE
SEE YOU BEAMING.

WHAT DID THIS POEM MEAN TO YOU
AND WHY?

. . . .

. . . .

. . . .

. . . .

SET YOUR HEART'S INTENTION FOR TODAY

. . . .

. . . .

. . . .

. . . .

"WHEN YOU'RE GOING THROUGH
SOMETHING HARD
AND YOU START WONDERING
WHERE ALLAH IS,
JUST REMEMBER...
THE TEACHER IS ALWAYS
QUIET DURING A
TEST."

USTADH NOUMAN ALI KHAN

"YOU ARE NOT A DROP
IN THE OCEAN.
YOU ARE THE ENTIRE
OCEAN,
IN A
DROP."

RUMI

"NOTHING IS IMPOSSIBLE.
THE WORD ITSELF
SAYS
I'M POSSIBLE!"

AUDREY HEPBURN

THOUGHTS ARE POWERFUL

WHENEVER MY MIND
RUNS LIKE THE WIND
AND MY THOUGHTS
JUST KEEP CREEPING IN,
I SIT PATIENTLY WISHING
UPON THE STARS,
BECAUSE I KNOW
IN MY HEART, WHENEVER
YOU SEE THAT SPARK
IN THE DARK, IT WILL
NEVER BE UNCLEAR,
THAT THE WISH
IN MY HEART IS CRYSTAL
CLEAR,
I JUST WANT YOU TO BE
HERE.

WHAT DID THIS POEM MEAN TO YOU AND WHY?

....

....

....

....

SET YOUR HEART'S INTENTION FOR TODAY

....

....

....

....

GROW IN SILENCE

THE SKY IS SILENT, THE WIND IS
GUIDANCE,
THE TREES GROW,
WHILE THE LEAVES BLOW,
RAIN WILL FALL
BUT THE SUN STANDS TALL,
DARKNESS OVERTAKES
THEN THE MOON SHOWS ITS FACE
YOU SEE
LIFE WILL CHANGE,
YOU MIGHT JUST STUMBLE
MAYBE EVEN CRUMBLE,
BUT ALWAYS STAY HUMBLE
YOU SEE AFTER THE FALL
YOU WILL ALWAYS
STAND TALL.

WHAT DID THIS POEM MEAN TO YOU
AND WHY?

. . . .

. . . .

. . . .

. . . .

SET YOUR HEART'S INTENTION FOR TODAY

. . . .

. . . .

. . . .

. . . .

"ALLAH'S TIMING IS PERFECT
IN EVERY MATTER.
WE DON'T ALWAYS UNDERSTAND
THE WISDOM BEHIND IT.
BUT WE HAVE TO LEARN TO
TRUST IT."

SYED NASIR HUSSAIN

LIFE'S HARDEST LESSON

FORGIVENESS IS HARD TO COME BY,
WE ALL TALK ABOUT IT
BUT RARELY ACT UPON IT
SO MY WISH TO YOU
IS THAT YOU LEARN
TO FORGIVE
BUT FOR YOU
THEN YOU WILL SEE
JUST HOW BEAUTIFUL
LIFE CAN BE,
BECAUSE FORGIVING YOU
IS ULTIMATELY
FORGIVING ME,
AND THAT IS WHAT WILL SET YOU
FREE.

WHAT DID THIS POEM MEAN TO YOU
AND WHY?

. . . .

. . . .

. . . .

. . . .

SET YOUR HEART'S INTENTION FOR TODAY

. . . .

. . . .

. . . .

. . . .

"WHATEVER THE MIND CAN
CONCEIVE AND BELIEVE,
IT CAN ACHIEVE."

NAPOLEON HILL

"DO NOT LET YOUR DIFFICULTIES
FILL YOU WITH ANXIETY.
AFTER ALL,
IT IS ONLY IN THE DARKEST
OF NIGHTS
THAT THE STARS SHINE
MORE BRILLIANTLY."

IMAM ALI (AS)

"THE BIGGEST ADVENTURE
YOU CAN TAKE
IS TO LIVE THE
LIFE OF YOUR
DREAMS."

OPRAH WINFREY

"SUCCESS IS NOT FINAL,
FAILURE IS NOT
FATAL; IT IS THE
COURAGE TO CONTINUE
THAT COUNTS."

WINSTON CHURCHILL

THE OCEAN'S CALLING ME

THERE'S SOMETHING UNDENIABLY
MAGICAL AND ALLURING ABOUT
THE OCEAN
TO ME, A SENSE OF CALMNESS IT
BRINGS ME,
AND HUMBLES ME
GRACEFULLY,
THE OCEAN HOLDS SO MUCH
POWER,
MAYBE EVEN
ANGER,
BUT IT'S A PLACE WE ALL WISH
WE COULD GO
WHEN WE'RE FEELING LOW,
TO LET OUR THOUGHTS FLOW,
AND JUST LIKE THE TIDE COMES
UP HIGH,
IT WILL SOON BALANCE INTO A
PERFECT HARMONY,
AND THAT'S WHAT I LOVE WHEN
THE WATER
SURROUNDS ME.

WHAT DID THIS POEM MEAN TO YOU
AND WHY?

....

....

....

....

SET YOUR HEART'S INTENTION FOR TODAY

....

....

....

....

SECRET PROMISES

THE STAR SHINES BRIGHT AND DEEP,
BUT HE HAS PROMISES
TO KEEP,
SO AS HE WISHES HER A GOOD
SLEEP,
HE WHISPERS IN HER
EAR,
YOU'RE MY PROMISE
THAT I HOPE TO KEEP,
MY LOVE FOR YOU RUNS
EVER SO DEEP.

WHAT DID THIS POEM MEAN TO YOU
AND WHY?

. . . .

. . . .

. . . .

. . . .

SET YOUR HEART'S INTENTION FOR TODAY

. . . .

. . . .

. . . .

. . . .

"IF WORKING APART
WE ARE A FORCE POWERFUL
ENOUGH TO
DESTABILISE
OUR PLANET,
SURELY WORKING
TOGETHER
WE ARE POWERFUL
ENOUGH TO
SAVE IT."

DAVID ATTENBOROUGH

"EVERY SAINT
HAS A
PAST,
AND EVERY
SINNER
HAS A
FUTRE."

OSCAR WILDE

CONNECT

LIFE IS A BLESSING
WHICH IS OFTEN OVERLOOKED,
BUT
IF WE REALLY PAY ATTENTION AND
CONNECT ALL THE DOTS,
WE COME TO REALISE
HOW MESMERISING LIFE CAN BE,
AND JUST KNOW
THAT IN THIS MOMENT YOU ARE EXACTLY
WHERE YOU'RE
MEANT TO BE.

WHAT DID THIS POEM MEAN TO YOU
AND WHY?

....

....

....

....

SET YOUR HEART'S INTENTION FOR TODAY

....

....

....

....

KNOW YOURSELF

SOMETIMES PEOPLE WILL JUDGE YOU,
DO NOT LET THAT
BREAK YOU
OR DICTATE THE PERSON
YOU KNOW YOU
ARE INSIDE,
LEAD WITH GRACE, HOLD UP THAT FACE
AND ALWAYS SPEAK WORDS
OF FAITH.

WHAT DID THIS POEM MEAN TO YOU
AND WHY?

. . . .

. . . .

. . . .

. . . .

SET YOUR HEART'S INTENTION FOR TODAY

. . . .

. . . .

. . . .

. . . .

FLOW LIKE THE WIND

WHY DO WE FIND IT DIFFICULT
TO LET GO
OF WHAT HURT US MOST,
IT IS OFTEN BECAUSE
WHAT HURT US MOST,
SHOWED US THE MOST LOVE WHEN
WE NEEDED IT,
BUT DO NOT LET
THAT FOOL YOU INTO HOLDING
ON TO IT,
REMEMBER
ONCE YOU LET SOMETHING GO
THE WIND ALWAYS HAS A WAY
OF RETURNING IT
BACK TO YOU IN SOME
SHAPE OR FORM.

WHAT DID THIS POEM MEAN TO YOU
AND WHY?

....

....

....

....

SET YOUR HEART'S INTENTION FOR TODAY

....

....

....

....

"WHAT DOES FEAR
TASTE LIKE?
SUCCESS,
I HAVE ACCOMPLISHED
NOTHING WITHOUT A
LITTLE TASTE OF
FEAR IN MY MOUTH."

BEYONCÉ

"STAY AWAY FROM
NEGATIVE PEOPLE,
THEY HAVE A
PROBLEM,
FOR EVERY
SOLUTION."

ALBERT EINSTEIN

"THE MOMENT ANYONE
TRIES TO
DEMEAN OR
DEGRADE YOU IN ANY WAY,
YOU HAVE TO KNOW
HOW GREAT YOU
ARE.
NOBODY WOULD BOTHER
TO BEAT YOU DOWN
IF YOU WERE NOT A
THREAT."

CICELY TYSON

TEST ME

ISN'T IT FUNNY HOW SOMETIMES
YOU FEEL LIKE THE GOOD
PEOPLE ALWAYS GET THE MOST
TESTS AND HURT IN LIFE,
AND IT FEELS LIKE THE PEOPLE
WHO DO WRONG
SEEM TO BE WINNING,
YES THAT IS WHAT I THOUGHT ALSO,
UNTIL
I REALISED, THEY ARE NOT WINNING
THE RACES,
BUT SIMPLY COMPETING
IN THEM,
STAY ON TRACK
SLOW AND STEADY
ALWAYS WINS THE RACE IN THE END.

WHAT DID THIS POEM MEAN TO YOU AND WHY?

. . . .

. . . .

. . . .

. . . .

SET YOUR HEART'S INTENTION FOR TODAY

. . . .

. . . .

. . . .

. . . .

SENDING LOVE

MY HEART IS FULL
OF LOVE TO GIVE,
NEAR OR FAR,
FRIEND OR NOT,
I'M HERE TO LEND A HELPING HAND
IN ANY WAY THAT I CAN,
SO I PICKED YOU TO
LEND A HELPING HAND
TO SPREAD
LOVE TO AS MANY PEOPLE
AS YOU CAN.

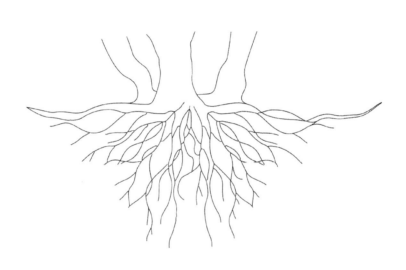

WHAT DID THIS POEM MEAN TO YOU
AND WHY?

. . . .

. . . .

. . . .

. . . .

SET YOUR HEART'S INTENTION FOR TODAY

. . . .

. . . .

. . . .

. . . .

"SELF-CONTROL IS STRENGH.
CALMNESS IS MASTERY.
YOU HAVE TO GET TO A POINT WHERE
YOUR
MOOD DOESN'T SHIFT BASED ON
THE INSIGNIFICANT ACTIONS OF
SOMEONE ELSE. DON'T ALLOW
OTHERS TO CONTROL THE DIRECTION
OF YOUR LIFE. DON'T ALLOW YOUR
EMOTIONS
TO OVERPOWER YOUR
INTELLIGENCE."

MORGAN FREEMAN

KEEP REACHING

DREAMS ARE THE BURNING
LIGHT INSIDE OF YOU,
WHAT MAKES US BELIEVE WE CAN
REACH FOR THE STARS
WHEN WE ARE YOUNG,
AND WHAT KEEPS US WANTING TO ACHIEVE
WHEN WE GROW OLDER,
NEVER LOSE
THAT INNER CHILD
WHO ALWAYS THOUGHT THEY
ONLY HAD TO
GROW A LITTLE MORE,
TO REACH THE STARS AND
THE MOON,
YOU'LL GET THERE SOON.

WHAT DID THIS POEM MEAN TO YOU
AND WHY?

. . . .

. . . .

. . . .

. . . .

SET YOUR HEART'S INTENTION FOR TODAY

. . . .

. . . .

. . . .

. . . .

UNDERSTATEMENT

FRIENDSHIPS ARE HARD TO COME BY,
IF YOU HAVE SOMEONE
WHO'S TRUE AND
ALWAYS THERE FOR YOU,
JUST KNOW
THAT YOU'VE HIT THE JACKPOT
BECAUSE THEY HAVE SOMEONE
WHO WILL ALWAYS
BE THERE FOR THEM TOO.

WHAT DID THIS POEM MEAN TO YOU AND WHY?

. . . .

. . . .

. . . .

. . . .

SET YOUR HEART'S INTENTION FOR TODAY

. . . .

. . . .

. . . .

. . . .

"WHILE THE MOST DANGEROUS
PERSON IN THE WORLD IS A
PERSON WITH NOTHING TO LOSE,
THE MOST POWERFUL PERSON
IN THE WORLD
IS A PERSON WITH
NOTHING TO PROVE."

TYLER PERRY

"I AM IN COMPETITION
WITH NO ONE.
I HAVE NO DESIRE TO PLAY
THE GAME OF
BEING BETTER THAN
ANYONE. I AM
SIMPLY TRYING TO
BE BETTER THAN THE
PERSON I WAS YESTERDAY."

SELENA GOMEZ

MY WORLD

MY FAMILY ARE MY EVERYTHING,
I MAY BE STUBBORN,
I MAY NOT EVEN SHOW
I CARE SOMETIMES
BUT IN THOSE MOMENTS WHEN I DO,
KNOW THAT IT'S EVER
SO TRUE
AND MY HEART WILL ALWAYS END UP
COMING BACK HOME,
BECAUSE EVEN
ROME
IS NO PLACE LIKE HOME.

*DEDICATED TO MY FAMILY

WHAT DID THIS POEM MEAN TO YOU AND WHY?

. . . .

. . . .

. . . .

. . . .

SET YOUR HEART'S INTENTION FOR TODAY

. . . .

. . . .

. . . .

. . . .

THERAPY FOR MY SOUL

MUSIC HAS ALWAYS BEEN MY ESCAPE,
AND MY SAFE HAVEN FROM
VERY YOUNG,
A FEELING I CAN'T PUT INTO WORDS,
THE MELODY, THE BEAT,
THE LYRICS
IT'S BEAUTIFULLY HARMONISED
TOGETHER,
IT TAKES ME TO A PLACE WHERE I FEEL
AUTHENTICALLY ME,
A PLACE OF EXPRESSION AND EMOTION,
FOR ME MUSIC WILL BE AND HAS
ALWAYS BEEN MY FIRST LOVE,
BECAUSE WHEN I FOUND MUSIC
I ALSO FOUND
ME.

WHAT DID THIS POEM MEAN TO YOU AND WHY?

. . . .

. . . .

. . . .

. . . .

SET YOUR HEART'S INTENTION FOR TODAY

. . . .

. . . .

. . . .

. . . .

"EVERY SITUATION IN LIFE
IS TEMPORARY. SO, WHEN
LIFE IS GOOD,
MAKE SURE YOU ENJOY
AND RECEIVE IT FULLY. AND
WHEN LIFE IS NOT
SO GOOD,
REMEMBER THAT IT WILL
NOT LAST FOREVER
AND BETTER DAYS
ARE ON THE WAY."

JENNI YOUNG

94

"IN A WORLD FILLED WITH HATE,
WE MUST STILL DARE TO HOPE.
IN A WORLD FILLED WITH ANGER,
WE MUST STILL DARE TO COMFORT,
IN A WORLD FILLED WITH DESPAIR,
WE MUST STILL DARE TO DREAM.
AND IN A WORLD FILLED
WITH DISTRUST,
WE MUST STILL DARE TO BELIEVE."

MICHAEL JACKSON

BLESSING

I AM SO BLESSED TO LOOK
AT YOU LIKE MY
MOTHER,
YOU MIGHT NOT KNOW THIS,
BUT I HOPE THAT YOU
NOTICE JUST HOW AMAZING
YOU ARE,
WHAT YOU HAVE DONE FOR ME
WILL NEVER LEAVE ME,
NOR BE FORGOTTEN EASILY,
YOU MAY NOT BE MY
BIRTH MOTHER,
BUT YOU ARE CERTAINLY
MY EARTH MOTHER.

*DEDICATED TO NADIA. S

WHAT DID THIS POEM MEAN TO YOU
AND WHY?

. . . .

. . . .

. . . .

. . . .

SET YOUR HEART'S INTENTION FOR TODAY

. . . .

. . . .

. . . .

. . . .

GRASS BETWEEN MY TOES

WHEN I CLOSE MY EYES AND
ALL I CAN SEE IS DARKNESS,
IT REMINDS ME OF HOW WE GET SO CAUGHT
UP IN THIS HECTIC WORLD SOMETIMES,
TO BE IN THE MOMENT
BUT REALLY IN THE MOMENT,
YOU HAVE TO TAKE YOURSELF
OUT OF EVERY
EQUATION,
JUST BE ONE WITH THE EARTH,
LET YOUR FEET TOUCH THE GROUND,
LET YOUR FINGERS FEEL THE AIR
BETWEEN THEM,
STOP AND REALLY SMELL THE FLOWERS,
ONLY THEN WILL YOU
TRULY FEEL AT
EASE.

WHAT DID THIS POEM MEAN TO YOU
AND WHY?

....

....

....

....

SET YOUR HEART'S INTENTION FOR TODAY

....

....

....

....

NOW

I DON'T WANT TO THINK ABOUT
TOMORROW,
NOR DO I WANT TO
THINK ABOUT YESTERDAY,
WHAT I DO WANT IS TO
LIVE FREELY IN THIS
MOMENT,
WHY YOU MAY ASK...
BECAUSE NO ONE CAN TAKE THE NOW
AWAY FROM YOU,
IT'S WHOLEHEARTEDLY YOURS,
DON'T WASTE IT,
MAKE THINGS HAPPEN!
I CAN SEE THAT SPARK IN YOU
EVEN IF YOU MIGHT NOT YET.

WHAT DID THIS POEM MEAN TO YOU
AND WHY?

. . . .

. . . .

. . . .

. . . .

SET YOUR HEART'S INTENTION FOR TODAY

. . . .

. . . .

. . . .

. . . .

"DON'T REGRET BEING
A GOOD PERSON,
TO THE WRONG PEOPLE.
YOUR ACTIONS SAY
EVERYTHING
ABOUT YOU,
AND THEIR ACTIONS
SAY EVERYTHING
ABOUT THEM."

VEX KING

8 WHEELS

ROLLERSKATING, IS SOMETHING
I HIGHLY UNDERESTIMATED,
THERE'S SUCH A BEAUTY ABOUT IT,
GLIDING THROUGH THE AIR,
ALMOST MAKES ME FEEL
LIKE A SUPERHERO,
IT'S LIBERATING AND
EMPOWERING,
ROLLERSKATING MAKES ME,
AND I CAN ASSURE YOU,
NEVER BREAKS ME.

WHAT DID THIS POEM MEAN TO YOU
AND WHY?

. . . .

. . . .

. . . .

. . . .

SET YOUR HEART'S INTENTION FOR TODAY

. . . .

. . . .

. . . .

. . . .

ONE OF ONE

IF I COULD CHOOSE ANYONE,
I'D KEEP CHOOSING
YOU,
BECAUSE NO ONE HAS THE SAME
HEART THAT I HAVE SEEN
IN YOU,
YOU ARE SPECIAL TO ME NO DOUBT
THAT'S TRUE AND THAT'S WHY
NO MATTER WHAT HAPPENS
IN LIFE,
MY FIRST CHOICE WILL ALWAYS
STILL BE YOU.

WHAT DID THIS POEM MEAN TO YOU
AND WHY?

. . . .

. . . .

. . . .

. . . .

SET YOUR HEART'S INTENTION FOR TODAY

. . . .

. . . .

. . . .

. . . .

"INNER PEACE DOES NOT USUALLY
LOOK LIKE BEING
PERFECTLY BLISSFUL
OR BEING PRISTINELY
CALM,
MORE OFTEN IT IS THE AWARENESS
THAT TOUGH EMOTIONS
ARE MOVING THROUGH
YOU WITHOUT GIVING THEM
CONTROL,
YOU FEEL THE CHAOS,
CHOOSE NOT TO GIVE
IT ANY FUEL,
AND INTENTIONALLY MOVE
GENTLY THROUGH YOUR DAY."

YUNG PUEBLO

LIFE LESSONS

TEACH TO EMPOWER,
READ TO LEARN.
FOLLOW TO DIRECT,
AND LISTEN TO UNDERSTAND,
YOU CANNOT ACHIEVE GREATNESS
WITHOUT STARTING
SMALL,
REMEMBER THE BIGGEST
ACCOMPLISHMENTS,
COME FROM JUST HAVING
ONE SMALL IDEA.

WHAT DID THIS POEM MEAN TO YOU
AND WHY?

. . . .

. . . .

. . . .

. . . .

SET YOUR HEART'S INTENTION FOR TODAY

. . . .

. . . .

. . . .

. . . .

"I DON'T LIKE TO
GAMBLE,
BUT IF THERE'S
ONE THING
I'M WILLING TO BET
ON,
IT'S MYSELF."

BEYONCÉ

"NOT IN DOING
WHAT YOU LIKE,
BUT IN LIKING WHAT
YOU DO,
IS THE SECRET
OF HAPPINESS."

J. M. BARRIE

"IF YOU WANT SOMETHING
YOU HAVE NEVER
HAD,
YOU MUST BE
WILLING TO DO
SOMETHING YOU HAVE
NEVER DONE."

THOMAS JEFFERSON

WORK OF ART

BEING A WOMAN IS MY POWER,
THE WAY MY BODY WAS PERFECTLY
DESIGNED TO BE THE CARRIER
OF ANOTHER SOUL,
THE WAY MY BODY MOULDS,
AND THE SCARS I HAVE TO SHOW
FOR IT AFTER,
THEY ARE WHAT SHOWS A WOMAN'S
TRUE STRENGTH,
AND POWER,
HER SCARS TELL A BEAUTIFULLY UNWORDED
STORY
A PICASSO PAINTING IS BEAUTIFUL,
BUT A WOMAN IS
UNDENIABLY MAGNIFICENT.

WHAT DID THIS POEM MEAN TO YOU
AND WHY?

. . . .

. . . .

. . . .

. . . .

SET YOUR HEART'S INTENTION FOR TODAY

. . . .

. . . .

. . . .

. . . .

LEFT WONDERING

DREAMS FLOATING,
LIKE THE OCEAN,
THEY COME AND GO
SO QUICKLY,
ISN'T IT WEIRD HOW THE MOST
AMAZING DREAMS
WE OFTEN CAN'T SEEM TO REMEMBER,
I WONDER WHY,
MAYBE IT'S BECAUSE
IT WAS NEVER MEANT TO BE REMEMBERED,
BUT ONLY FELT,
WITHIN THE HEART.

WHAT DID THIS POEM MEAN TO YOU
AND WHY?

. . . .

. . . .

. . . .

. . . .

SET YOUR HEART'S INTENTION FOR TODAY

. . . .

. . . .

. . . .

. . . .

SIDE BY SIDE

TAKE MY HAND,
HOLD IT TIGHT,
EVERYTHING WILL BE ALRIGHT,
YOU'LL ALWAYS HAVE ME
BY YOUR SIDE,
I PROMISE I WILL
BE YOUR GUIDE,
AND IF I CAN'T BE THERE
PHYSICALLY,
I'LL ALWAYS BE THERE
SPIRITUALLY.

WHAT DID THIS POEM MEAN TO YOU
AND WHY?

. . . .

. . . .

. . . .

. . . .

SET YOUR HEART'S INTENTION FOR TODAY

. . . .

. . . .

. . . .

. . . .

"ACCEPT RESPONSIBILITY
FOR YOUR LIFE.
KNOW THAT IT IS YOU
WHO WILL GET
YOU WHERE YOU
WANT TO GO,
NO ONE ELSE."

LES BROWN

"YOUR BEST IS FAR BETTER
THAN YOU CAN IMAGINE.
YOU CAN DO FAR MORE THAN
YOU THINK YOU CAN.
DO NOT BE A MEDIOCRE
VERSION OF
YOURSELF.
GO OUT AND DO WHAT
YOU ONCE THOUGHT IMPOSSIBLE
AND RISE UP TO
A NEW LEVEL
OF ACHIEVEMENT."

CHRIS LESAK

GOD KNOWS

TRIALS AND TRIBULATIONS,
ONLY GOD KNOWS WHAT
I'VE BEEN THROUGH,
BUT WILL IT
STOP ME... NO,
WILL IT DESTROY ME... NO,
BUT WILL IT MAKE ME... YES,
THAT IS SOMETHING I AM MOST CERTAIN OF,
I MAY FALL 100 TIMES,
MAYBE EVEN 1000 TIMES,
BUT I'LL ALWAYS MAKE SURE
I'M DANCING WHILE I'M DOWN THERE
AND SINGING WITH MY MOP,
UNTIL ONE DAY,
I MAKE IT TO
THE VERY TOP.

WHAT DID THIS POEM MEAN TO YOU
AND WHY?

. . . .

. . . .

. . . .

. . . .

SET YOUR HEART'S INTENTION FOR TODAY

. . . .

. . . .

. . . .

. . . .

#BLM

THE WORLD NEEDS US,
STAND TALL, DON'T FALL,
YOU SEE ALL OF THESE RULES ARE
HERE TO FOOL,
BREAK AND TEAR US APART,
WE HAVE TO UNITE
AND FIGHT FOR WHAT'S ONLY
RIGHT, DESPITE WHAT'S HAPPENING
TONIGHT,
I PRAY WE NEVER LOSE
SIGHT OF WHAT'S TRULY RIGHT,
BLACK OR WHITE
UNDERNEATH OUR SKIN,
WE ALL BLEED THE SAME COLOUR,
AND IF YOU DON'T
UNDERSTAND THAT,
THEN MAYBE YOU'RE JUST A...

WHAT DID THIS POEM MEAN TO YOU
AND WHY?

. . . .

. . . .

. . . .

. . . .

SET YOUR HEART'S INTENTION FOR TODAY

. . . .

. . . .

. . . .

. . . .

THE DEFINITION

I AM YOU,
YOU ARE ME,
TOGETHER WE CREATE
THE PERFECT HARMONY,
FLOATING ON AIR WITHOUT A CARE,
LOOK AT THE WIND
BLOWING GENTLY THROUGH
YOUR HAIR,
YOU ARE LOVE'S DEFINITION,
AS SIMPLE AS CAN BE,
IT WILL FOREVER BE,
YOU AND ME.

WHAT DID THIS POEM MEAN TO YOU AND WHY?

. . . .

. . . .

. . . .

. . . .

SET YOUR HEART'S INTENTION FOR TODAY

. . . .

. . . .

. . . .

. . . .

FULL MOON

JUST LIKE THE MOON
LIFE IS ALWAYS FULL,
IT JUST DEPENDS ON WHAT YOU SEE
AND WHAT ANGLE YOU ARE
LOOKING AT THINGS ON,
NO MATTER HOW MUCH OF THE
MOON YOU SEE ON CERTAIN NIGHTS
ALWAYS REMEMBER BEHIND
THE CLOUDS
THE MOON IS ALWAYS FULL
AND BRIGHT,
IT JUST DEPENDS ON THE
ANGLE YOU CATCH ON
THAT VERY NIGHT.

WHAT DID THIS POEM MEAN TO YOU
AND WHY?

. . . .

. . . .

. . . .

. . . .

SET YOUR HEART'S INTENTION FOR TODAY

. . . .

. . . .

. . . .

. . . .

"IT'S EASY TO STAND
IN THE CROWD BUT IT
TAKES COURAGE TO
STAND ALONE."

MAHATMA GANDHI

LIST YOUR TOP FIVE FAVOURITE QUOTES THAT SPARK A LIGHT IN YOU...

1.

2.

3.

4.

5.

Milton Keynes UK
Ingram Content Group UK Ltd.
UKHW050839021023
429768UK00008B/47